THE BIG BOOK OF
BAD
DATES

SELLERS
PUBLISHING

Published by Sellers Publishing, Inc.

Sellers Publishing, Inc.
161 John Roberts Rd.
South Portland, Maine 04106
For ordering information:
(800) 625-3386 toll free
Visit our Web site: www.rsvp.com • E-mail: rsp@rsvp.com

President & Publisher: Ronnie Sellers
Publishing Director: Robin Haywood
Managing Editor: Mary Baldwin
Senior Editor: Megan Hiller
Assistant Production Editor: Charlotte Smith
Cover Design: Heather Zschock

ISBN: 13: 978-1-56906-989-9

10 9 8 7 6 5 4 3 2 1

Printed and bound in India.

THE BIG BOOK OF
BAD DATES

**The Not-So-Good, the Very Bad
& the Butt Ugly**

written & illustrated
by JO RENFRO

The Shyster

The Pretty Boy

The Village Idiot

The Guy's Guy

The Old Hippie

The Bad Sweater Guy

The Downer

The Type A

The Mom's Choice

The Rich Guy

The Pink Guy

The Tightwad

The Desperado

The Perpetual Partier

The Youngster

The World Traveler

Contents

Introduction

Remember when dating was fun? There were plenty of singles to go around and an abundance of men to choose from. We used words like "hottie," "flat belly," and "nice butt" to describe our conquests.

As the years passed, the pool of single guys began to shrink, and our married friends instead tried to fix us up with guys whose descriptions included words like "balding" and "paunchy." Of course, the matchmakers bolstered these potential date descriptions with words like "good hygiene" and "a really nice personality."

We either held firm to our high standards, which often resulted in no dates at all, or we began to flex a little on our rigid requirements. Things like employment became much more important, and things like appearance became slightly less important (but only slightly). (Shallow . . . maybe, but at least we're honest!)

With these lower standards come a lot of hilariously ridiculous dates, and the dating dandies in this book are just a few of the Mr. Absolutely-NOT-Rights you might encounter (if you haven't already).

The Big Book of Bad Dates will bring a smile to the face of every woman who has ever had to sprint to her front door to avoid an unwanted kiss at the end of an especially disastrous date.

— *Jo Renfro*

Dating Tip #72

The Fake Phone Call. You have a friend call at a predetermined time. If the date is an absolute disaster, this is the perfect escape. Family emergency. Gotta run!

Chapter One

He means well . . . *really*

The Wild Man

This guy is crazy. He's constantly on the move. Just what you need, right? He's funny, he's loud, he's fit, he's active, he's daring, he's adventurous. He's . . . a little scary maybe?

He means well . . . *really*

You go tandem skydiving with **The Wild Man**. A friend gets a shot just as you are about to hit the ground and comments on how much fun it looked like you had. Fun? That is sheer terror on your face.

12

The things we do for love.

He means well . . . *really*

13

You go out for ice cream with **The Wild Man** and are surprised when he orders a plain vanilla cone! Pretty boring! Until you come across the latest study on ice cream and personality types — Vanilla: Colorful, impulsive, and a risk taker. Figures.

15

The World Traveler

This guy has traveled the world. Sort of. He's been to 21 of the contiguous United States and Mexico. Once. On spring break in college. He has style and sophistication. Just ask him.

16

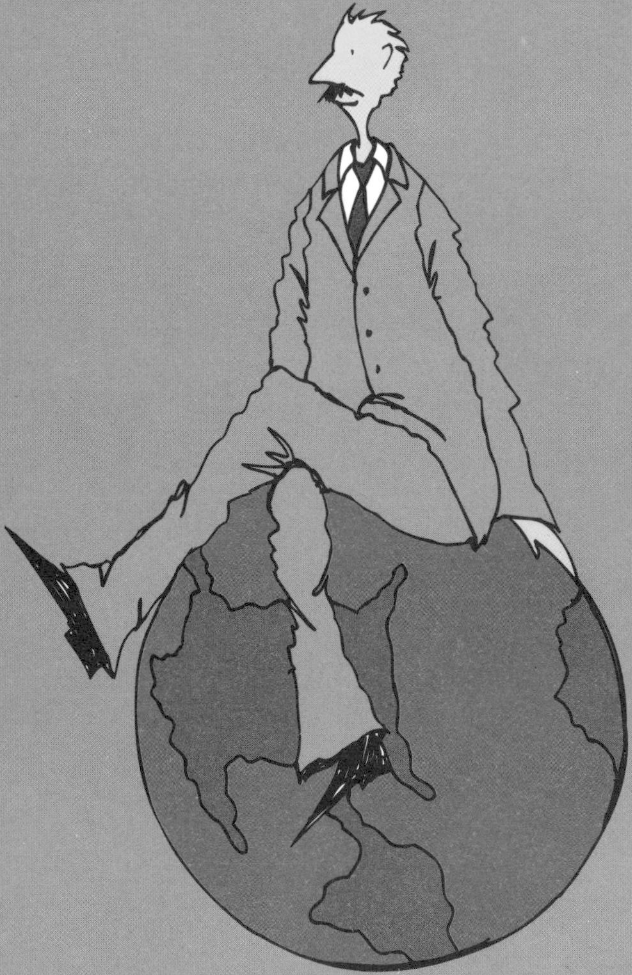

The World Traveler shows you photos from some of his travels. First up, a shot of him with the World's Largest Ball of Twine. Yee ha!

He means well . . . *really*

The World Traveler is wearing full safari attire. On his way to Kenya? Nope, to the movies with you. Maybe only slightly embarrassing?

20

He means well . . . *really*

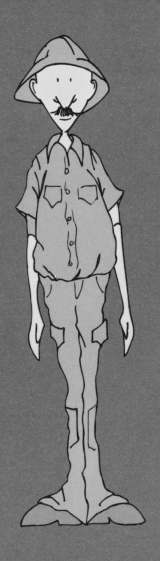

21

The Pseudo Athlete

Shiny new tennis shoes and a matching velour sweat suit. Ask him what sport is his favorite and he says, "Tossing the old pigskin through the hoop." Turn and run if you meet this guy. He'll never be able to catch you.

23

You run into **The Pseudo Athlete** at the gym. He spends his time sipping power drinks and chatting with anyone who will listen. This guy *never* breaks a sweat.

24

Tennis with **The Pseudo Athlete**. He's got all the right gear and looks great until he actually tries to hit the ball. He takes a shot to the face and has all the coordination and quickness of a three-legged turtle.

27

The Type A

Before you even climb in his car, he opens the trunk, where he's stored an industrial-size case of handy wipes. He asks you to wash your hands and remove your shoes before you climb into his spotlessly clean car. Don't even bother!

28

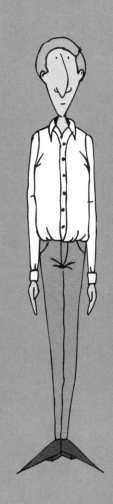

29

You have a date with **The Type A**. He always smells just slightly of cleaning solution. Does he mistakenly think that 409 is cologne?

He means well . . . *really*

You see **The Type A** at a party and he's dancing! Wow! Actually, he is swaying back and forth with barely perceptible movements, fists clenched tight, but hey — he's trying!

32

33

The Klutz

A faceful of roses, a finger smashed in the door, a poke in the eye when he goes to brush your hair back from your face. Is he worth the risk? Talk about living dangerously.

35

He means well . . . *really*

You make a serious error in judgment by mentioning a burned-out light bulb when **The Klutz** comes to pick you up. Being the nice guy that he is, he insists on changing it before you go out for dinner. You end up spending the evening dining on candy bars from the hospital vending machine.

36

38

The Downer

He's also known as The Eternal Pessimist. Continually in therapy (or maybe he should be). Not only is his glass half empty, it's evaporating so fast he may as well not even bother taking a drink. He could wipe the smile off the Mona Lisa.

39

You run into **The Downer** at the airport on the way out of town, and he's complaining about how much baggage he has. You chuckle to yourself. Too much baggage. That's an understatement!

40

42

Finally it's Friday and you are ready for some fun!

The Downer asks you to join him for a drink because

he's feeling a little sad. Maybe a night on the couch,

alone with a quart of ice cream doesn't sound so bad.

Or cleaning the toilet. Or scrubbing the bathtub . . .

43

The Has-Been

He's living in the past — his old football glory days.

Even though that was 15 years and 75 pounds ago.

44

46

The Has-Been invites you to come watch him play in a pickup game with some of his old cronies. As the ball nails him on the back of the head and nearly knocks him out, you pretend to be fumbling in your purse in search of some elusive object, to save everyone a lot of embarrassment.

He means well . . . *really*

In desperation, you call **The Has-Been** to accompany you to your company holiday party. He shows up in a tasteful, charcoal suit, but screaming from underneath is his old jersey! You feign a sudden illness and retreat to the couch.

48

He means well . . . *really*

49

Dating Tip #37

Caller I.D.
Get it!!!

Chapter Two

A man among men

The Guy's Guy

Your first date is an evening at his favorite tavern for

a night of beer, darts, and pickled eggs. OK, I guess.

But when you get home, instead of a kiss, you get a

slap on the back like an old army buddy.

53

A man among men

The Guy's Guy asks you to play a little one-on-one. OK. You're a fun gal who's always up for a little physical activity. But when the guy checks you as he drives to the basket, you wonder if he's even aware that you're a female.

55

The Guy's Guy pegs you with a 90-mile-an-hour snowball in the back of the head. This guy has got to go!

57

The Practical Joker

He's a real knee-slapper. Everything's a joke to this guy. *Everything!* You can't even walk down the street without fearing he'll pop out and scare the heck out of you. Very funny.

60

WHOOSH

The Practical Joker takes you out to your favorite restaurant. Very nice, until you sit down on the whoopee cushion he has strategically placed on your chair. It could be a long night.

61

After a long night with **The Practical Joker** and his really bad jokes, you arrive home with a fake grin permanently cemented on your face. Your cheeks actually hurt from fake smiling.

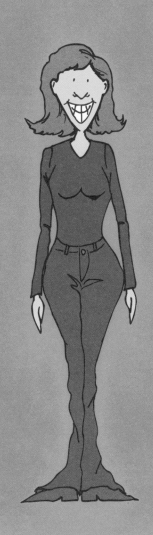

The Urban Cowboy

You think you've met a real live cowboy. He has all the

trappings. Boots and a tobacco-can circle worn in the

back pocket of his tight jeans. Until he tells you he's

from Cleveland, and the only horse he's ever ridden

(for a quarter) was in front of the local grocery store.

You should have known when his ten-gallon hat was

about nine gallons too big for his head.

A man among men

You attend a black-tie event with **The Urban Cowboy**.

Well, shucks, Sheriff. His bolo tie is black, isn't it?

67

68

"He's a nice little filly," says **The Urban Cowboy** as he pats your dog. You're no horse expert, but isn't a filly a girl?

69

The Dancing Fool

Fool being the operative word. Once you hit the dance floor, he only has eyes for himself. A few too many hours spent practicing in front of the mirror at home, perhaps?

70

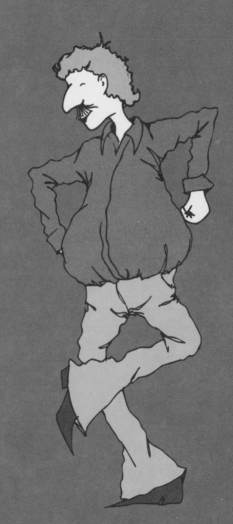

72

A night out dancing with friends, so you invite **The Dancing Fool**. What were you thinking?! He can't wait because he has some new "moves" to try out. Apparently, he has the words "moves" and "spasms" confused!

73

The Dancing Fool joins in on a round of the limbo. He wants to see how low he can go. You wonder if maybe you are setting the bar a little too low yourself.

74

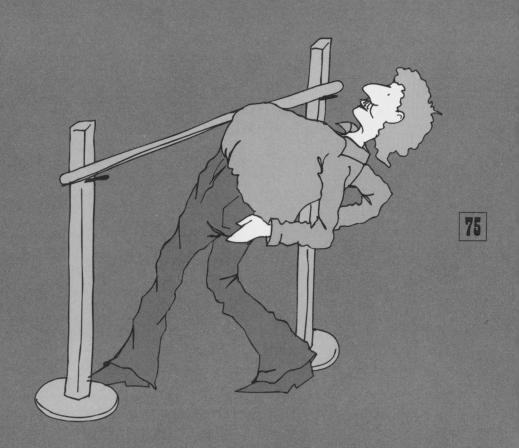

The Maniacal Fan

You meet him through a friend at halftime of a basketball game. He seems like a nice enough guy, and he asks you to go to dinner with him on Saturday. Sure! Why not?

The Maniacal Fan invites you to go to a major league baseball game, and of course, he's wearing the team jersey. And he's bringing his glove. And he's wearing his cleats. Why does the word "wannabe" keep flashing in your head?

78

80

While curled up watching the news on TV one night, you see an incident at a recent sporting event. Omigosh! It's **The Maniacal Fan** being hauled out of the arena after getting into a brawl with the opposing team!

81

The Drunken Dialer

It's midnight. He calls to say he can't stop thinking about you (even though you only had one date six months ago), and he wants to stop by for a "hug." Well, he can't stop thinking about *something* anyway.

83

84

You cave in and go on an actual date with **The Drunken Dialer**. After bringing you home, he tries to kiss you with all the passion and sophistication of a St. Bernard. Gross!

85

The Drunken Dialer shows up at your house, reeking of whiskey, and nearly falls in face first when you open the door. Now isn't that sexy?

86

A man among men

88

The Perpetual Partier

He's a tight-jean, gold-chain-wearin' guy. Mid-40s and he still spends his weekends at Party Cove in his Speedo.

The Perpetual Partier stops by for a drink. Have we even touched on the fact that this guy has a mullet straight out of some 1980s TV sitcom?

90

91

A night out with **The Perpetual Partier**. You're going to prove (to whom?) that you can still party with the best of them. But when the trash can full of jungle juice appears, you have flashbacks to nights spent hanging over the commode, and you make a swift exit. Party on, dude.

93

It's your worst nightmare. All of the men you've dated this year are standing at your door, and you're told you have to pick one to spend the rest of your life with. *Aaaugh!* Thank goodness it *is* only a nightmare!

95

Dating Tip #33

The Fake Dropped Call.
This is the beauty of cell phones.
Not quite sure how to get out of a
bad conversation? The fake dropped
call works every time.

Chapter Three

All he needs is love

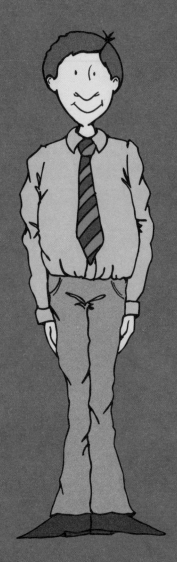

The Nice Guy

He calls when he says he will, and he's thoughtful and kind. This is the guy we *should* date but probably never will.

All he needs is love

The Nice Guy calls you for a date. When he arrives,

you notice a few little sprouts on his face. He says

he's trying to shake up his nice guy image. Oh, you

have to admit it's sort of cute, but those three little

100   hairs on his chin just aren't doing the trick.

All he needs is love

101

102

A date with **The Nice Guy**. He says he'll be there to pick you up at 7:30 and he is. You open the door and there he is, holding a bouquet of your favorite flowers. Daisies. Is this guy annoying or what?

103

All he needs is love

The Nice Guy invites you out for a drink in yet another attempt to shake up his good guy image. After an entire beer (almost), he passes out cold. Let's face it — once a nice guy, always a nice guy.

All he needs is love

105

The Mom's Choice

Every mother has someone she just *knows* is the perfect guy for you. She constantly tries to set you up with him. And it's usually someone like your Aunt Ruthie's friend's cousin's nephew, Herbie . . . No thanks, mom.

107

All he needs is love

Your mom invites you over for dinner and lo and behold, look who just happened to stop by. It's **The Mom's Choice**. What a coincidence. Actually, it feels a little more like an ambush!

110

Your mom finally guilts you into going out with **The Mom's Choice**. And to karaoke night, no less. *Ouch!* And he's not kidding! You spend the entire evening in the ladies' room with your ears plugged. *Way* too embarrassing!

The Mamma's Boy

Easy to spot. Asks you out for Friday night because that's the night he gets his allowance. Starts each sentence with, "My mom says. . . ."

All he needs is love

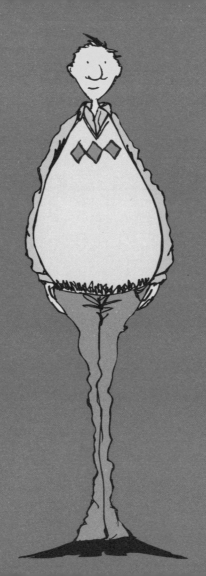

113

The Mamma's Boy takes you home (Mom's home, that is) to meet his pet fish, "Swimmy." Geez. How old is this guy?

115

You stop by **The Mamma's Boy**'s house to drop off the jacket he left in your car. He answers the door seemingly unaware that it's not considered normal for men his age to be wearing blue, footed pajamas.

All he needs is love

The Mamma's Boy invites you over for a home-cooked meal. He forgot to mention that it would be cooked by Mom. As the three of you sit down to dinner, you begin to plot your escape.

All he needs is love

The Space Invader

He's not happy unless he's groping, stroking, or squeezing you 24/7. In the car, in the grocery store, at dinner parties, and at sporting events. He's all over you like a bad bottled tan. Personal space? This guy's never heard of it.

All he needs is love

122

At an event with **The Space Invader** and a few friends, he sequesters you at the far end of the row, away from the group. You plot your escape. Would it be rude to knock him out of his seat and trample him as you run for freedom?

123

You've discovered that *The Space Invader* is allergic to cats. Ha! Is it wrong to use your cat as a shield?

124

125

126

The Desperado

This guy *really* wants a mate. He's an instant boy-friend. Just add water. As long as you're a living, breathing female, you're the gal for him!

All he needs is love

The Desperado says he has something to tell you. He's falling in love with you. Say what? You've never even gone out with the guy! I mean, you know you're good, but this is ridiculous!

All he needs is love

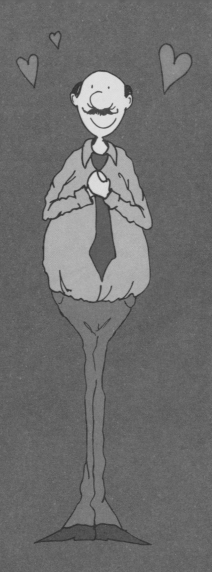

129

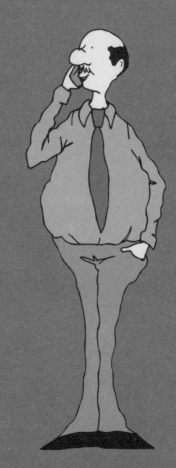

130

The Desperado calls to tell you he's been thinking about you and misses you so much. Your head starts to swell just a little bit, due to his obvious love for you, but you turn him down once again. He doesn't miss a beat as he asks for the phone number of your friend Gina. Your head deflates quickly, as you realize once again that he loves any woman who will speak to him.

131

All he needs is love

You just want to go shopping at the mall without the risk of running into these disastrous dates. Do you really think a fake nose and glasses will fool anyone?

132

133

Dating Tip #26

Transportation. Be sure to have your own! At least until you're sure you want to spend time with this guy! This ensures a quick, easy escape.

Chapter Four

Looks like a winner

136

The Pretty Boy

He has thick, gorgeous hair, beautiful skin tone, ruby red lips . . . wait a minute! Do I *really* want to be "out-prettied" on a date?

It's your birthday and **The Pretty Boy** wants to stop by with your gift. It's *perfect* he gloats! Maybe that new scent you mentioned wanting?? Nope, it's a framed 8x10 glossy of him. Gee, what a thrill.

138

While sitting at dinner with **The Pretty Boy**, you notice he has something green in his teeth. Are you good and politely point it out, or evil and keep your mouth shut and enjoy every embarrassing second? For once, good does not prevail. *Hee hee hee.*

141

The Youngster

He's cute. He's fun. He's fit. He's got a job. He's at least ten years younger than you are. But he's interested in you. Should you be flattered or freaked out?

Looks like a winner

143

144

The Youngster gets a raise at work and asks you to join him for a drink to celebrate. You think wine. He means beer bong.

145

You run into **The Youngster** and as you turn to go, he accidentally says, "Bye, Mom." *What?!* He laughs it off, but you don't. You turn and *run* at a dead sprint. You are much too young and fabulous

146 to be his mother. *Right?!*

147

148

The What-in-the-Heck

This guy sends some seriously mixed signals. One minute he can barely keep his hands off you and the next he's complimenting you on your accessories and asking to borrow your new pashmina.

Looks like a winner

You attend an outdoor concert with **The What-in-the-Heck** and it begins to rain. He's soaking wet, and you offer him some dry clothes. He comes out in a pair of pink capris with a matching floral tank top, claiming it's all he could find that would fit him. How about the sweatpants and T-shirt you'd laid out for him? *Hmmm . . .*

150

151

152

*The **What-in-the-Heck*** comes by to go for a hike.
He's wearing old, holey jeans and a manly flannel
shirt. Hmmm. Maybe you were wrong about him. But
something is different. Is that eyeliner he's wearing?

153

The Bad Boy

He drives too fast, never calls when he says he will

(if he calls at all), and barely remembers your name.

Of course we love this guy!

155

The Bad Boy calls (an hour after he was supposed to be there to pick you up), and says he's feeling a little under the weather and is just going to stay home on the couch. Is that music and laughter you hear in the background? It must be the TV. Denial at its finest.

157

You run into **The Bad Boy** at a party. He says hi and then turns and walks away. It's a good thing he has a nice rear end, or you'd drop him so fast it'd make his head spin. That'd show him. Yeah, right.

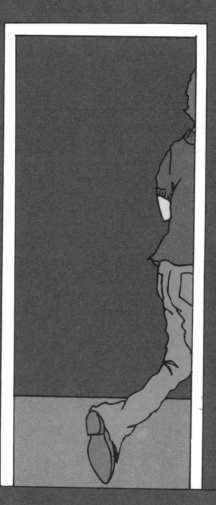

160

The Old Hippie

This guy is permanently stuck in the '60s. He's cool, he's laid-back, and yes, you'd even say he's groovy. Maybe it's a good thing. Or maybe it's not. Time will tell.

161

You go to listen to a band with *The Old Hippie*. Wow! It's so smoky! It's so loud! Do they really think this is music? It's really just a bunch of noise. Shock sets in. When did it happen? How did it happen? You have

162 gone over to the dark side. You feel officially old.

163

The Old Hippie invites you to go hang out at a park with him. You need to relax more. He immediately falls asleep in the grass while you sit restlessly beside him. You tell yourself relaxing is good, relaxing is good, relaxing is good. Relaxing is about to drive you insane as you run screaming from the park.

165

The Just-My-Luck

He's handsome. He's engaging. He's funny. He's

intelligent and he dresses impeccably. Of course.

He's gay.

167

NOW SHOWING
STEEL
MAGNOLIAS

Movie night with **The Just-My-Luck**. Your favorite

and his, *Steel Magnolias*.

169

At dinner with **The Just-My-Luck**, you get into a heated argument over who the hot, attentive waiter, Paulo, is interested in. You or him. Paulo slips his number to your dinner friend, answering the question once and for all. It figures.

170

DATING STANDARDS

172

REQUIRED FIELDS

- ☐ SENSITIVE
- ☐ ADORING
- ☐ GIVING
- ☐ KIND
- ☐ FUNNY
- ☐ THOUGHTFUL
- ☐ SEXY
- ☐ SMART
- ☐ CHARMING
- ☐ ATTRACTIVE
- ☐ EMPLOYED
- ☐ INTERESTING
- ☐ PHYSICALLY FIT
- ☐ ADVENTUROUS
- ☐ FUN

EXTRA CREDIT

- ☐ IMPECCABLY DRESSED
- ☐ TOTALLY HOT
- ☐ FILTHY RICH
- ☐ INCREDIBLY HANDSOME
- ☐ NAMED GEORGE CLOONEY

Do you think you're being too picky? Heck, no!

Dating Tip #9

Involve friends. That way, if you end up going out with some big goofball, you can laugh with them and say, "What were we thinking!" Spread the blame. Strength in numbers.

Chapter Five

Who is this guy?

176

The Clueless Guy

This guy has no idea that you are interested in him, no matter how obvious you try to make it. Calling, dropping by his house, baking his favorite cookies. Some might call it stalking, but he appears totally oblivious!

Who is this guy?

You've invited **The Clueless Guy** over for "dinner" (wink wink) and open the door wearing the sexiest, little black dress you own. He comes in and says politely that he can't wait to see what you're serving because he's starving. He really expects dinner! You dash into the kitchen and whip up some boxed macaroni and cheese. That's impressive.

Who is this guy?

The Clueless Guy is *not* picking up on any of your subtle hints that you are interested in him! What do you have to do?? Wear a signboard announcing it to the world. I mean, how stupid would that be? Hmmm . . . I wonder where they sell those things.

181

The Rich Guy

Big money, big house, big car, big spender, big ego,

big jerk. But, he has money . . . so we can put up

with a little jerkiness.

Who is this guy?

184

The Rich Guy comes by to pick you up and he is wearing an animal! A big, full-length animal! Do you go, even though you are against the fur thing, or do you take a stand and refuse to accompany him? Hmmm. However, you *are* hungry . . .

185

You go to the casino with **The Rich Guy**. On the way in, you pass a group of kids selling candy bars from their school. **The Rich Guy** refuses to buy any, saying he doesn't have any money on him. Inside the

casino, he slaps down a couple hundred dollars on a long shot without blinking an eye. Nice guy, eh?

187

The Rules-Don't-Apply

The only rule for this guy is there are no rules.

At least not for him. Politically correct is not in

his vocabulary.

189

Who is this guy?

At dinner with **_The Rules-Don't-Apply_** guy, he decides he likes the glassware, so he stuffs one in his jacket. Very classy.

The Rules-Don't-Apply guy calls to say thanks for fixing him dinner and that he forgot to tell you (although he knew you wouldn't mind) that he borrowed your toothbrush. The gagging begins immediately as you fling the toothbrush into the trash.

The Shyster

There's just something a little shady about this guy.

He always seems to be working an angle or making

a deal. He winks so often you begin to wonder if it

isn't actually an involuntary twitch.

194

195

The Shyster takes you out for a nice dinner with great wine and all the trimmings. Hmmm. Very nice, until you see him tear off a fingernail and throw it in his dessert and loudly demand that they comp your entire meal or he'll sue. Do you think anyone recognized your shoes as you hid underneath the table during this horrifying tirade?

197

Out to dinner with **The Shyster,** and he spends most of his time hunched over in the corner on his cell phone, speaking in a muffled voice to someone named Vinnie. You do your best not to eavesdrop.

198

The less you know the better.

200

The Bad Sweater Guy

Picture every color and texture known to humankind knit together in one giant wad of fashion disaster and you've got our man.

You attend a Fourth of July picnic with **_The Bad Sweater Guy_**. Maybe we should just change his name to the Bad Clothing Guy. I mean, come on! Isn't there something not right about actually wearing the flag?

202

203

The Bad Sweater Guy has asked you to a holiday dinner and brings you a special gift. A sweater with an almost life-size appliqué of Rudolf with a flashing red nose on the front. He insists that you wear it out to dinner. Nausea ensues.

205

Who is this guy?

The Tightwad

This guy is cheap. Frugal. Thrifty. Chintzy. Stingy. So why do you go out with him? Boredom? Insanity? Idiocy? Who knows!?

206

207

You see **The Tightwad** jumping around like a crazed maniac! He must have won the lottery! Wow! Nope. A new coupon book came in the mail with a coupon for the new place he's been wanting to eat at. At last, he can finally try it (because as we all know, you can't eat somewhere without a coupon).

The Tightwad is going to stop by for a drink and wants to bring you some of your favorite wine, just name it. When he arrives, he informs you that that flavor doesn't come in a box, so he chose something that was about the same color. Yummy.

210

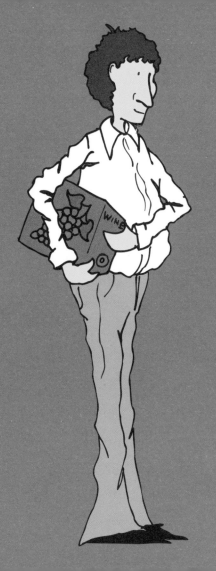

Dating Tip #43

Do you have to return a call from a bad date? Do it when you are certain that he isn't home, of course! That way, you've technically returned the call and yet avoided the uncomfortable confrontation.

Chapter Six

At least *someone* likes him

214

The Rooster

You meet him at a bar and before you can even introduce yourself, he's spewing out a stream of every impressive piece of information about himself that he can possibly think of. He goes for the "ta-da" type of first impression; it comes off more like a "thump."

You receive a newspaper clipping in the mail about **The Rooster** from **The Rooster**. Modesty is not his deal. You can't figure out if he's cocky or really insecure.

216

The Rooster invites you to listen to him play his horn at an upcoming open-mike night. He notes that you'll be amazed at how good he is! You can't help but smile when you see him up there tooting his own horn!

219

At least *someone* likes him

The Intellectual

This guy is smart. And well read. And well travel-ed. This could be just what you need to expand your horizons. But do you really want to have to study before you go out with him?

220

221

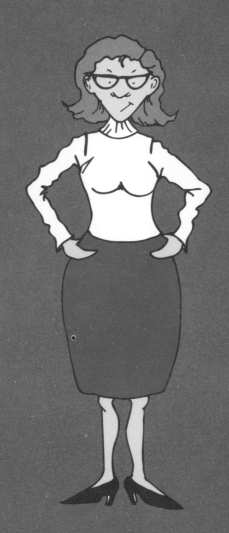

222

You have a date with **The Intellectual**, so to look smarter, you buy cheap glasses and wear a tasteful charcoal gray skirt. Wow. It is scary how much you look like your third-grade teacher Mrs. Getto. This is not a good thing.

223

The Intellectual invites you to come to a lecture he's giving. It's like listening to the grown-ups in the old *Peanuts* cartoons. Wa-wa-wa-wa-wa. A real snoozer! You make a quick escape afterward to avoid discussing his topic with him. Whatever it was!

At least *someone* likes him

225

The Know-It-All

He seems to know everything about everything. From politics to interior design. And he says he's so full of information it would boggle the mind. He's full of *something*, that's for sure.

At least *someone* likes him

Your sink has an annoying little drip and **The Know-It-All** won't let you call the plumber because he's sure he can fix it. No problem. Until the water is rocketing out of the faucet like Old Faithful. Now can you call a plumber?

The Know-It-All is *actually* trying to tell you your last name is misspelled. He thinks you should go through the proper legal channels to have it changed. Who is this guy? Is he crazy?

231

The Big Talker

Also known as the almost millionaire. Almost won the lottery, almost discovered a new, renewable source of energy, almost made the stock deal of a lifetime, almost got a job . . .

At least *someone* likes him

233

The Big Talker drops by to say hi, wearing some very expensive cologne. (Or so he says.) The scent arrives five minutes before he does, and there is a visible cloud surrounding his head. He just doesn't get the "less is more" thing.

235

At least *someone* likes him

Dinner out with *The Big Talker* at an expensive French restaurant. An evening filled with stories of lost fortunes. As the waiter delivers the check, *The Big Talker* reaches into his pocket, only to discover that he's forgotten his wallet. Surprise, surprise.

236

At least *someone* likes him

237

The Village Idiot

He laughs too loudly and talks too much, certain that everyone at the restaurant wants to hear his fascinating account of the time his dog barfed up an entire squirrel. Speaking of barfing . . .

239

At least *someone* likes him

You go to the movies with **The Village Idiot,** and he proceeds to talk through the entire thing! People around you are complaining, but it doesn't even faze him. Would he even notice if you silently crawled away up the dark aisle?

At least *someone* likes him

You run into **The Village Idiot** while shopping. The entire time you're talking, he's smacking his gum and blowing giant bubbles. He's a talented guy. Very impressive.

The Vicious Circle of Dating.

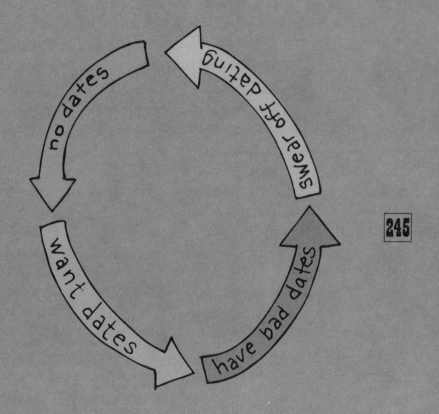

245

Dating Tip #12

Desperate to get out of a date? Just say the words, "I'm having 'women's issues.'" Code for "I'm having my period." This works 100 percent of the time. Trust me. He won't be able to get off the phone fast enough.

Chapter Seven

A fine, fine specimen

The Missing Link

Is he man or beast? You could braid the hair on his

back. If you're into that sort of thing. Ooooh.

You attend a modern art exhibit with **The Missing Link**, but you can't focus on anything but the hair poking out of the back of his sweater. Loose knits just don't seem to work well on this guy. Why do you keep thinking about Chia Pets?

A fine, fine specimen

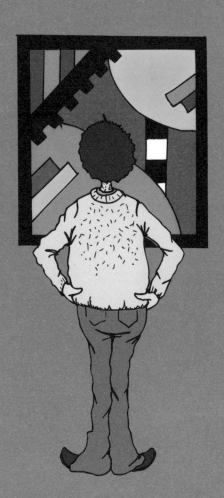

251

7 p.m.   11 p.m.

You attend a horror movie marathon with **The Missing Link.** When the lights come back up after four hours in the dark, you scream in sheer terror! Not because of the movies, but because your date has become the werewolf!

253

The Carpet Guy

No, this is not his profession. It refers to the rug he has pasted on top of his head. You try to look him in the eye, but your gaze just keeps drifting north. It's like when you see roadkill: you don't want to look, but you can't stop yourself. Is that thing dead or alive?

A fine, fine specimen

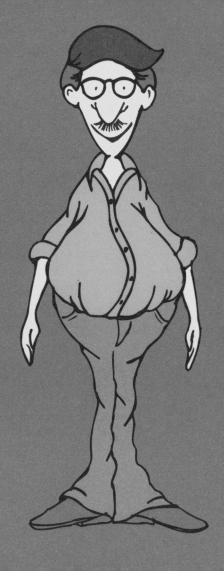

255

256

You run into **The Carpet Guy** and he has a new rug.

He's gone from plush to shag!

257

The Carpet Guy is discussing the new rug he's going to get. Red with a tone-on-tone pattern. You have a hard time getting a visual of a patterned "rug," but you're impressed with how candid he is about his hairpiece. It's not until he mentions that it will be 8x10 that you realize he's talking about an actual rug.

258

A fine, fine specimen

259

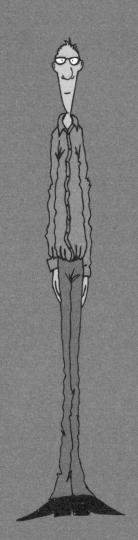

The Thin Man

Come on! We all know we can't date a guy we can out-eat, out-arm-wrestle, and whose jeans are smaller than ours!

A fine, fine specimen

Hiking with **The Thin Man** today. It was great, except for the one moment of sheer panic when you thought you were lost in the woods *alone*. Turns out, he was right there beside you the whole time. He just blended in with all the other twigs.

263

You run into **The Thin Man** at the gym. This is the first time you've seen his legs exposed. Yowsa! They are half the size of your forearms! This is not a good thing.

265

The Strong Man

Are those bones you hear breaking as he rubs your shoulders? Gentle is not in his repertoire. And do we really want to date a guy with bigger breasts than ours?

266

267

You've heard of "cankles" (when calves and ankles are almost indistinguishable from one another). **The Strong Man** has a "nead," in which his head and neck almost appear as one.

A fine, fine specimen

You have a hard time getting motivated to go to the gym, but you arrive just in time to see **The Strong Man** have a wardrobe malfunction. Pink ladies' underwear?!! Definitely worth the trip to the gym.

The Pink Guy

Soft and squishy are the words that come to mind.

Shaking his hand is like squeezing a water balloon.

You just want to curl up with this guy (and use him

as a pillow).

273

A fine, fine specimen

Cooking "in" with **The Pink Guy** and he can't get the jar of pickles open, so he hands it to you. You ask yourself who the man is in this relationship, and you're not crazy about the answer.

274

The Pink Guy invites you to go Christmas tree shopping with him. It's not until it's time to load it that he mentions his recent back injury. It's then that you realize why he actually brought you along. Oh yeah. You're going to hoist that tree somewhere, but it may not be on top of his car.

The Comb-Over

He seems like a nice enough guy, but why does he have those four strands of hair brushed strategically over his obviously balding head? Who is he trying to fool?

279

You meet **The Comb-Over** for dinner at a lovely restaurant downtown. He looks great, except he seems oblivious to the fact that static electricity has set in and his "hair" is standing at attention on top of his head! Do you embarrass him and tell him, or just pray that eventually it just falls into place on its own?

A fine, fine specimen

You run into **The Comb-Over** on a particularly blustery day. He has a death grip on those three hairs plastered across his bald head. You want to scream, "We know you're bald!!! Relax!," but you manage to restrain yourself.

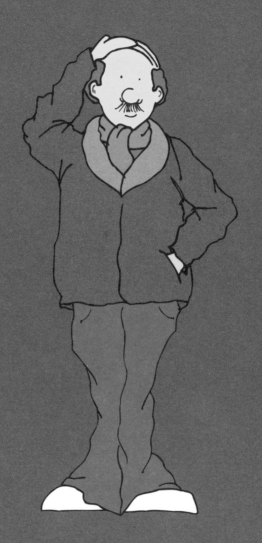

Epilogue

You swear off dating forever and plan to spend the rest of your life happily fraternizing with your loyal dog. Unconditional love. No more dates. Never, ever again. And then, the phone rings . . . could it be . . .

285

The Perfect Guy

He's funny, charming, handsome, kind, thoughtful, athletic, and engaging. He loves talking, cuddling, and walks on the beach. He loves your friends and they love him. He's not married, not gay, and he . . .

doesn't exist!